Basic Life with Rhonda Gayle
Book Series

Be a Wife & Mom While Making $ with Affiliate Programs!

Rhonda Gayle Turner Garner

Be a Wife & Mom While You Make $ with Affiliate Programs!

DEDICATION

I dedicate this book to my parents, my Dad, RET. SFC John Ray Turner (April 18, 1921 – July 6, 2003), I miss you Daddy, and my Mom, RET. Florence School District 4 Teacher and Food Service Coordinator, who is still very much a major part of my life and without her, I wouldn't be where I am today. Thank you Mom for Being the Woman I have written about. And most of all, thank you for ALL of your SACRIFICES.

To my husband, Jerome Anthony Garner, who with and through the six years of marriage, GOD-FATHER LOVE has shown me the VALUE of Patience, through – LIFE, Christ Jesus, HIS SON. I love you and appreciate your VALUE. May you EVOLve continuously into the man you are DESTINED and PURPOSED to BE!

I also accredit Pastor John S. Battle (former NBA player with Cleveland Cavaliers and Atlanta Hawks) and his wife, 1st Servant Minister Regina Belle-Battle (Grammy Award Winner – Regina Bell) for not only "teaching" me but "showing" me HOW to "long suffer" which is a quality of LOVE that most seem to forget these days. I thank you and appreciate you both for allowing me to experience this first hand.

To my SIX...
IV, Trinity, Le'Andre', JhondaRaye, J'Lindan & Jakobe
John – Mommy loves you and I AM proud of you all!
May you ALWAYS FOLLOW the path of LOVE – LIFE
& TRUTH and Maintain Excellent Health, Healthy
Wealth, Wealthy Wisdom with Ultimate Favor to
have and be VERY PRODUCTIVE, PROFITABLE and
LUCRATIVE in ALL that your put your Hearts, Minds
& Souls to DO!

To my other Mother – "Mama Dean" – May
COMFORT & JOY be unto you THIS day and ALL of
your days to follow to lead you continuously on the
path of LOVE, LIFE and TRUTH that will Equip,
Empower, and Evoke you to BE who you ARE... and
that is LOVED!

To my Friend & Business Partner, "Jaaaye", no words
can ever express my gratitude and appreciation for
you and ALL that you have done and sacrificed for
my family and myself... Know that no matter what
anybody else may say...

To my Cousins, my In-Laws, my Relatives, my
Friends, my Clients, my Customers, my Social Media
Followers and my Supporters... Thank you all for
helping me to BE the person I AM today...

I LOVE YOU ALL!

Disclaimer

This publication is intended to provide helpful and informative material. It is not intended to diagnose, treat, cure, or prevent any mental, emotional, financial or physical issues, problems or conditions, nor is intended to replace the advice of any Specialist in said areas. No action should be taken based solely on the contents of this book. Always consult a specialist or qualified professional on any matters regarding your mental, physical, financial or emotional health and well-being before adopting any suggestions in this book or drawing inferences from it.

The author and publisher specifically disclaim all responsibility for any liability, loss or risk, personal or otherwise, which is incurred as a consequence, directly or indirectly, from the use or application of any contents of or references in this book.

Any and all product names referenced within this book are the trademarks of their respective owners. Not any of these Advertisers, Founders, or Owners have sponsored, authorized, endorsed, or approved this book.

Always read all information provided by the manufacturers' products, services, and/or labels before using their services or products. The author and publisher are not responsible for claims made by any advertisers, owners, or manufacturers.

TABLE OF CONTENTS

ACKNOWLEDGMENTS

Audrey Bell-Kearney, HerTube.TV
Georgette Taylor, HerTube.TV
FonTonya Myrick, Heal and Grow, LLC
Julius Williams, Jr., Williams Tax Service
Hampton Institute University Alumni
Williams*AdnohR Tax Service Clients
Amazon.com / ACX.com
The Authors, the Producers & the Write Holders who have chosen and those who choose to have me to Narrate for them.
Roku.com
CJ Affiliate by Conversant
GoDaddy.com
All of my Social Media Followers
To the Supporters and Patrons of The AdnohR Connection and all of its Divisions
American InterContinental University Online, Buckhead, GA
Macedonia Living Word Fellowship – Cincinnati, OH
Greater Faith World Outreach Ministries – Florence, SC
Overflowing Fountain Ministries – Lamar, SC
New Shield of Faith Christian Ministries – Atlanta, GA
HootSuite.com
Walter Lee Younger, the Extraordinaire – Black Folk Inc.
Zipp Transportation Inc., Allison Zenelish Hickson, Founder & CEO
Fiverr.com
Google
Social Media – FaceBook, Twitter, Linkedin, Google+, etc.

1ST
CHAPTER

WHERE TO START

Where do I start you may ask? Well, because I wanted to be able to offer a variety of things, information and sources to my clients, customers and patrons, I looked to Commission Junction which is now known as CJ Affiliate by Conversant. They offer a wide range of "name brand" Advertisers not only to choose from but to partner with. Initially, I would go from company to company, scroll down to the bottom of their website's Home Page and click on the "Affiliate Program" link. Now I was doing this from company to company by "searching" the company's name; however, I found that most of the companies use CJ Affiliate by Conversant or the link directs you to the CJ website, anyway, so to avoid a waste of time, I just signed up directly for CJ Affiliate by Conversant and applied to all of the companies at one time.   Simple.

Now, I am also an Amazon Affiliate as well. I became an Amazon Affiliate first because I desired to become an Author (*this was way before I knew that Amazon sold products)* and Amazon was known to me as "the" company that Authors sold their books. So even before I knew that amazon had an "affiliate program" I was searching Amazon.com to see what services I could utilize as an Author. Well, in my research, I found that Amazon sold products and that you could "link" to these products as an "affiliate" and that's what I did. So, Amazon and CJ Affiliate by Conversant are the two platforms I am set up wih as an Affiliate.

Affiliate programs are a great way to earn extra income and the two major ways that I do is one, I shop my "advertisers" personally, whether setting up my auto maintenance through Firestone or buying an automobile through the Yahoo Affiliate banner I have on my website, I get paid!

And second, I created a "Banner Shopping" page on my website! However, in this day and age, of course, Social Media is one of the greatest ways to promote your Advertisers! One of my dearest and closest friends, who I also call my Sister, FonTonya Myrick, Founder and CEO of Heal and Grow, LLC, which consists of Hair and Scalp nutrition with the BIOSTRAND products (facebook page – HealandGrowHair) as well as Coaching and Consulting – *(which is really an understatement in her repertoire and arsenal of information that she has in her portfolio of business experience)* - suggested that I join and sign up for HootSuite, which will enable me to post my Affiliate links to all my Social Media pages at one time! And it works wonders! Therefore, to get it out there all at once so that you won't have to go back and forth to each of your pages *(and I have many)* ... sign up for HootSuite.com!

Where to start, as for me, it hasn't been "un-challenging", because I have had to "be all" to "everyone"... Encourager/Minister, Entrepreneur, Wife, Mother... you name it, getting everything together to start in building an Affiliate Business took some "trial and error" and I am still making every effort to "smooth out the bumps".

Because of the vast changes in technology, upgrades, apps, etc., I want to be "up to date"; however, that sometimes make room for and causes "inconsistencies"; therefore, if you do choose an Affiliate Company that offers a "variety" of Advertisers, then you should only "upgrade" your Affiliate Business, when the Advertisers upgrade or change their ads. Because otherwise, you will find yourself all over the place.

2ND
CHAPTER

NOW THAT YOU HAVE SIGNED UP AS AN AFFILIATE, WHAT NEXT?

Okay, now that you are an official Affiliate, what comes next? Well, if you haven't already, you must create a BLOG or a WEBSITE, I have both. Now what I suggest so that you get "paid", make sure that you have been APPROVED as an Affiliate first with the Web Hosting Advertisers – like GoDaddy, Yahoo

Small Business, Host Gator, Certified Hosting, just to name a few *(these use CJ Affiliate by Conversant)* - that you are going to use to build your website from. Also use their banner or link on your site as well, copy and paste your affiliate link from your APPROVED Web Hosting Advertiser into your web browser and that will bring up your affiliated Web Hosting Advertiser's website. Now, after you sign up or purchase your website hosting account, you will get "paid" or "commission" for your first sale... you! And most "hosting" companies pay big commissions for sales; therefore, remember:

- **Become an Affiliate FIRST!**
- **Then make PURCHASES through YOUR Affiliate links or Banners!**

I, actually did this step backwards and lost out on a "healthy" commission! Oh, well, you have the advantage now, so I must reiterate – APPROVED AFFILIATED HOSTING ADVERTISER, FIRST, "then" PURCHASE your WEBSITE through *YOUR OWN AFFILIATE LINK!*

Choose your business

Okay, now, what is your business? Not sure? Well, that's okay, that is why I wrote this book, because I am a Business Developer as well. Let's start here...

- What is your Passion?
- What is it that you ENJOY doing that NO ONE has to "force" you to do?
- What is that you love to do even if you didn't get paid for it?
- What, if money was NO option, would you be doing?
- What is it that you believe that you can do "better", even if someone else is already doing it?
- What drives you, motivates you, inspire you?

Well, THAT'S your business, that is what you should "be about"... that is what you "should be" getting paid for. And if done with the drive, the passion and the consistency that I know you possess, you will not only be SUCCESSFUL "at" it, but you will get WEALTH "from" it!

So, let's say that you chose the business of cooking. Now what you would want to do is choose Affiliate Links such as those Advertisers who sale or promote cooking and all that evolves around cooking. And if you are a Mother of small children like myself, you would want to involve links or banners for them as well. Links and banners such as:

- Cookware
- Kitchen
- Food Clubs
- Toys
- Educational and/or Instructional Material
- Childcare
- Furniture
- Automobiles for Catering
- Uniforms, costumes, etc.

And these are just some of the Affiliate Link banners and/or links that you use and promote on your website for your cooking business. You want to "strategically" place them where they will be noticed as you build your website. You may check out mine at: **http://www.theadnohrconnection.com**. – The AdnohR Connection!

3RD
CHAPTER

BUILDING YOUR WEB OR BLOG SITE(S)

Unless you are a pro at html or any of the other "back door" web building entities... I suggest TEMPLATES! Templates are your friend! I use GoDaddy, because they have everything, right at your fingertips *(not to say that the others do not)*; however, GoDaddy allows me fast, easy and convenient site building tools that I don't have to spend a lot of time trying to figure out. Everything is right there! And because one of my businesses is business development, which includes website designing and website maintenance for my clients, GoDaddy is easier for me to maintain everyone's site.

Now, if you choose CJ Affiliate by Conversant for your Affiliate programs, what I like to do is, first go to the Advertisers tab to find out which advertisers I have been approved for to be an Affiliate with. Let's go back and set up which links to choose for your cooking business website. On the left hand side, I choose the "My Advertisers (Active)" Status then click SEARCH to get my links. In doing this, all of "my" approved and active Advertisers are sorted and that way I will only have the links and banners that are approved and active to use. This is done so that you are NOT using an "inactive" Advertiser on your site, because if the Advertiser is "inactive" you won't get paid any commission for any banner/link clicks, leads, or sales, so REMOVE any "inactives"; however, keep an eye opened if and when they REACTIVE their status. Also, if you have other Advertisers that you may not use on your cooking website, that's okay, use them on your site as well. Also, if you go back to the left side of your screen, under the "Category" section, you can actually "search" your links in "categories" which will help you just choose from the "category (ies)" you wish to place on your site. The eMails from your Advertisers will keep you abreast of any promotions, sales, offers along with their ADR or active/deactivated/reactivated status information.

Now, BLOGS are also great to place banners in, especially if you just don't want to use a website or you would just prefer blogging. I like to type, write and talk; therefore, blogs are perfect for me; however, I do like websites as well, because of the various designs and outlines they provide. So, I do both; however, that depends upon the time and attention that you have, to allot to either. Blogging, because I like to write, sometimes is a little more time consuming, because of the husband and the children are constantly "not knowing where anything is" or "they are hungry and like no one else in the house knows 'how' to cook but me (being sarcastic)"; hence, I only get to blog either early in the morning or after everyone is in bed.

Taking time and consideration, you must set aside TIME as to when you can build and/or maintain your web and/or blog site, because it is "deserving" of the same time and ATTENTION as your, spouse and children, because THIS is YOU... THIS comes from your soul; therefore, to financially provide, sustain, empower and equip you and your family, you must either work your business as a "part-time" or "full-time" career! Treat your business and your home office as if you were "literally" leaving your home, taking transportation, driving or fighting crowds, etc., to go into a "brick and mortar" building. If you use your mind, time, and space like that your business will be a success and in doing so, YOU will be REWARDED, emotionally, spiritually, mentally and financially!

MARKETING & ADVERTISING

Congratulations, you are now the proud owner of a business with a website, as well as an Affiliate with some of the major companies in the United States of America and across the globe! Your business is global! You now have the potential of becoming Internationally known! Well, now what?

Okay, now, what you will want to do is Market and Advertise your business for Financial Income and Gain, as well as, provision for your family, not to mention those shopping sprees!

Marketing

What is marketing? According to Google, *mar·ket·ing ˈmärkədiNG/ noun - the action or business of promoting and selling products or services, including market research and advertising.* How do you want to get your business out there to others? Who is your "target market"? Will you be a "Soul Food" Cook that will take the "traditional" soul food dishes to the next level, such as "Healthy Heart Smart Soul Food" or maybe even "Vegetarian Soul Food"? What time of "taste buds" will you want to appeal? The possibilities are limitless, because you have been empowered by your Creator to imagine, design and create something that you are passionate about and only "you" hold the answer to!

Because of technology, you definitely have to use Social Media to cover ground you couldn't otherwise cover in the timeframe that it takes to click a few links and push a few keys. Something that you can pretty much, set, and forget. Now because I have a "financial diet" that doesn't incorporate me utilizing "major" marketing firms or campaigns for my company, at the moment, I do research and find economically sound companies and campaigns that offer "30 day free trials" or "Free Basic" tools that are easy to use that will enable me to DIY... "do it myself". Also, it is "recommended" that even with DIY campaigns through platforms such as, Yahoo, Facebook, Google, you should spend at the very least $1.00 per day on your campaign. However, at the moment, my "financial diet" doesn't call for that in my program.

Now as aforementioned, I use "HootSuite", because they enable me to access all of my Social Media platforms right there all together and also gives me the ability to "send them out" with just a few simple clicks! Also, I can "schedule" how many times I would like my Affiliate Links or Website/Blog site(s) to "appear" or "stream" to my Social Media pages at any given day of the week *(I just schedule the "most" times, every day of the week)*; therefore, HootSuite has me pretty much going 24/7 and I just update my content each week! Hence, set it and forget it!

Now, if your financial budget is more of that which will enable you to "splurge", then these are the areas you really want to concentrate −

Marketing and Advertising – which are your "money making" twins. With a nice budget of, let's say five to 20 thousand dollars per month, you will be able to "do" just about any Social Media Marketing & Advertising Strategy Campaign out there.

Advertising

Aren't they the same? If not, what is Advertising? Well, let's go again to Google... *ad·ver·tis·ing ˈadvər͟tīziNG/noun - the activity or profession of producing advertisements for commercial products or services, i.e., "movie audiences are receptive to advertising",* and that's why I called them "twins", because you really can't have one without the other. By what "means" or what "platforms" will you utilize to "show off" your business? Social Media is one way; however, please incorporate at least one or two of the others, such as:

- Print – Newspapers, Magazines, Newsletters, Business Cards, etc.
- Visual – Television, Video, Billboards, Signs, DVD, etc.
- Audio – Radio, CD. Telephone, etc.
- Internet – Social Media, Click Sites, Search Engines, etc.

And remember, this should be the MAIN portion of your BUSINESS BUDGET, because without proper Marketing and Advertising, sorry to say that your business is pretty much, "dead in the water". '

Oh, and by the way, the GREATEST Marketing and Advertising tool that beats the others "hands down" is... WORD OF MOUTH! Word of mouth and "referrals" is what I've used for years, especially in my Income Tax Preparation business. Offering incentives, prizes, tickets, gift cards, etc and of course excellent Customer Service will sky rocket any business venture. I will cover that more a little later.

5TH
CHAPTER

RESEARCH IS ACTUALLY THE 1ST STEP

Actually, RESEARCH is the VERY 1ST step in ANY successful business *(along with trial and error),* and not to mention "failure"... yes, I did say "failure". Corporate giants didn't get there overnight, and neither will you; however, remember when you answered the questions about "what" your business should be in the first place, and you answered that it was something that you "loved" to "do" anyway and it is something that you would do for free? Well, that's the catch to ANY SUCCESSFUL person, place or thing... PASSION. If you are working your business solely JUST to "make money", you're going to fail. TRUTH is, it has to come from the heart, it has to come from the place of "wanting better" for your family, friends, clients, customers, neighbors, neighborhood, community, county, city, state, nation, country, world, and the people thereof, including yourself, in order make a difference. Of course you may not be able to change the world; however, you are able to make great changes in your family and in yourself that will exude and radiate your passion from within, and THIS is what makes the difference!

When others "see" the very thing that you are passionate about, they not only want to "get on board", but they will "pay" for it as well. Look at the businesses around you. Research "how" they all started. It wasn't just from an "idea", but it was from someone wanting to "make a difference", "make a change" in their circumstances and/or situation, whether it was, financially, physically, emotionally, socially, or mentally. So I reiterate... What is it that YOU want to change? What is the one thing that you would be doing if you weren't concerned about MONEY or TIME? If you had all of the money that you needed and all of the time that you wanted to put into that "burning" desire what would it be? Okay, let's do this... back to cooking.

There are tons of television shows about cooking, and I am pretty sure that they all have websites, so, go to the "About Us" tab on their web or blog site and if you have a cookbook around, go to the "About the Author" page and that should tell you as to "why" they got started in the "cooking" business in the first place, why cooking is their passion.

Also, find news articles or go to the websites of one of the ingredients that you would like to use and pull up the company that makes that ingredient and read about the company, their financial projection and their history. This will not only give you clarity and insight about the ingredient/product, but how and why that ingredient/product was chosen in the first place. What makes it so special.

Research Yourself

Everything that is anything starts with "self". Once you know yourself, you will know your passion and once you know your passion, you will "know" what "business" you are to "be about". Get someplace quiet to reflect. Whether good, bad or ugly, you will find out what you want to change, rearrange, or capitalize on and "why", and that will make the difference in your life.

Great people, places and/or things came and comes from someone's pain or pleasure. Someone wanted to share their pain or their pleasure and make a difference. You are no different. Even the pain that you may have experienced can be shared and capitalized upon to make a POSITIVE difference not just in your life, but in the lives of others. Although, another is not you, most people share similarities, in spite of their differences. It doesn't matter if they are of the same race, background or even spiritual beliefs, because of humanity, there is someone out there in the universe who has gone through or will experience that which you may already have. No, maybe not on the same level or at the same magnitude; however, similar and/or relatable. So much so that they would not only be willing to patronize your business, but be a repeat, returning, life-long client or customer. So, don't be afraid to share your experiences, because in doing so, you will find your passion.

6TH

CHAPTER

WORD OF MOUTH

Communication is key in any relationship, business, social, professional, etc.; therefore, Word of Mouth promotion is essential. Start with your family and friends. Call them, eMail, write them, tweet them, or even gather them together under one roof, to share your great and wonderful news!

Advise them that you are now an Affiliate with some of the major companies that "they" do business with and now they can do business with those same companies, except now, they can do business "through" you! Email them the Affiliate links or direct them to your website or blog and ask them if they would be so kind as to now shop through your Affiliate links and banners. Let them know that with some of the Advertisers, they will be able to "save" time and money, because most Advertisers give online discounts and with some of the major ones, you will be able to "buy' online and then "pick-up" at the store and that way they will just have to "pick-up" their order, instead of going from isle to isle to shop, avoiding traffic, crowds and long checkout lines. They are now able to "shop" from the comforts of their own homes and patronize your business at the same time!

Remember, as you "spread the word", make sure that you pass out your business cards *(give at least two so that your potential client/customer will have one to keep and one to share)*, thus, enabling them to "spread the word" about your product and/or services. If you have any "incentives" in place, mention those up front to get them excited about your business. Maybe give a discount if their "referral" mentions your business or business card in the comment section of your blog or website, or if they leave a comment with a 5 star rating they can get a free product or service. There are many ways to generate "word of mouth" and this is where "trial and error" come in to play. Just keep adjusting your approach and technique until you find which way is best for you.

Make sure to check your Affiliate eMails often, because you will be able to find great sales and promotion from the Advertisers that you can offer as a promotion, discount or incentive. Share with your potential and existing clients or customers that when they purchase your product or service, you can give them the link for a sale or discount from one of your Affiliates and that way, when the sale is completed, you can either eMail them your Affiliate link or use the link as a "landing page" for that discount or special. *(A landing page is a page that directs customers to a specific place, website, or page that you would like them to view, or "land" after their order is placed).*

Landing pages can also be used if they "start' an order; however, they change their minds and decided not to order your product; however, they can still be "directed" to your Affiliate site and if they purchase from there, you will still get the credit or the commission. This is great for Advertisers who pay for "leads", because they really don't have to make a purchase if they are a qualified lead for the Advertiser to contact later. You will still get "paid" for that "lead" and potential customer for that Affiliate *(CJ Affiliate by Conversant have Advertiser who also pay for leads, this will be listed beside "Network Earnings" column under the "Advertisers" tab)*.

Remember, even if you have multiple businesses, word of mouth will vary according to what business you are promoting at the time, because your clientele will be different with each business. One person may love and enjoy your "cooking" business; however, another may choose to patronize your "sewing" business *(not to intentionally put cooking and sewing together; however, it just came out that way)*. Therefore, you must prepare for, and run each, not only separately, but differently. Even if you just have the one company, but different "divisions" of the company, each division must be "prepared for", "executed" and even operate differently from each other.

7TH

CHAPTER

PROPER PREPARATION AND EXECUTION

A lot of planning and preparation must be involved to balance your roles as an individual and an Entrepreneur. If you haven't done so already, it's now time for scheduling. Calendars, organizers, notes, day planners, etc., are going to be essential to pull this off and be the success that it can and will be "if" you "stick to the plan". Sure, plans may go array; however, PREPARATION is key in the event of any "unexpected" changes, challenges or events. "LIFE" does and will happen and when it does, don't let worry, frustration, fear, doubt or disbelief set in. Just rearrange, adjust and change some things to take a different route or approach to what you are wanting to accomplish for that day.

Keep in mind, "ONE DAY AT A TIME". If you are not able to accomplish that which you had hoped for that day, rearrange or regroup some things to do it later on that day or even another day. Don't try and "eat the whole whale" or "build the entire city" in one day. It's called "business BUILDING" and you're not even to the "foundation" stage, yet. Every building, home, business, etc., took and takes the "design" and "blueprint" stage even before the "foundation" is even laid. Planning and preparation and even the way it is executed take time and patience.

Even with earning an income with Affiliate Marketing, you will still have to prepare and schedule how you would like to "incorporate" and "execute" your Affiliate links. Having everything right there at your fingertips is all well and gravy; however, there has to be an order, timing, and system in place, too, that will properly prepare a successful execution of your links that will generate a momentum of continuing and repeat customers to create a consistent income base and will keep those commissions coming in that will create the wealth and provision for sustaining your family and yourself financially.

Write the Vision, Make it Plain

GOD's Word Translation – Biblehub.com - Habakkuk 2:
2) *Then the LORD answered me and said,* **"Record the vision And inscribe it on tablets, That the one who reads it may run.**

3) **"For the vision is yet for the appointed time; It hastens toward the goal and it will not fail. Though it tarries, wait for it; For it will certainly come, it will not delay.**

4) **"Behold, as for the proud one, His soul is not right within him; But the righteous will live by his faith....**

It doesn't matter "who" applies this, know that the "law of gravity" governs us all on planet Earth.

Sure, one may "defy" it momentarily; however, eventually, "what goes up, must come down". Well, the same goes for anyone who "writes and work" their vision. Here's the scripture in plain English – defined - Habakkuk Chapter 2:

- **Verse 2** – Then **LIFE** gave me or through **LIFE**, I had an epiphany... If I write down my ideas, my passion, that thing which I love doing if I see it, look at it and study it daily, I will in doing so, won't run from it, nor will I be afraid to make it a reality.
- **Verse 3** – I know that I will need to research my idea, prepare and organize my time and schedule my time to prepare to be able to make my idea into my reality. This will take time and patience, and if I make the time and take the time to properly prepare, and work my passion daily as I would on a job, or in a career, it will pay off. When I put in motion the research, preparations, schedule, patience, time and attention, my dreams will become my visions and my visions will become a reality.
- **Verse 4** – Those who "think" that it will "just happen" just because "I believe" that it will, or "I pray" that it will, without proper preparation, research, scheduling, time, attention, patience,

consistency, writing, outlining, etc., well... your "thinking" is not right; however, the successful lives by executing the "courage" to do the work in the building of the business.

Any idea that is given to you must "be" and you must "take" RESPONSIBILITY for. Prepare yourself with outlines, agendas, calendars, day planners, to-do-lists, journals, photos, pictures, etc., to keep yourself on task. Give yourself something to look at daily. Log into your eMails from your Affiliate platform(s) and your Affiliate platform(s) itself to view any changes, new promotions, sales, deactivations, new approvals, etc., to keep abreast of any Advertisers that you can incorporate or need to remove to keep that momentum of income coming in. Write these down or use your computer's note pad to copy and paste them to so that they will not be "out of sight and out of mind".

Especially, be very mindful of the sales the Advertisers are promoting, because these may just be "one day" sales, and if you do not promote that Affiliate link that day, you may miss out on the opportunity to make commission from that Advertiser. Sometimes, the Advertisers will just send you an eMail with a "special" link that you won't find on the actual Affiliate Program's platform, because these are "extra specials" that maybe the Manager or the company is doing as an added "bonus" for their Affiliates and their Customers.

Execution

Honestly, you may NOT be ready to execute or promote your business or Affiliate Program(s) until about three to six months from your initial "commitment" to actually even "start" working your business, especially if you gather the information, do your research, and properly prepare the materials needed to "successfully build" your business, which will lessen your "trial and error" experiences. Sure, you will still experience some trials and errors; however, not at the magnitude that you would have if you hadn't properly prepared.

Before publishing your web and/or blog site(s) and after you have gotten everything in place, do a *"coming soon"* or a *"premiere"* promotion about your business, website, blog, etc., on Social Media, your "word of mouth" advertisers *(friends, family, associates, co-workers)*, and any other advertising and marketing platform, about a week or two before your actual launch. Create a YouTube video that you can use for your "trailer" or "premiere" and direct people to your video. This will gather "feedback" for you that will enable you to correct, heighten, boost, rearrange or even scrap before you launch your business.

So, before you actually "release" and "show" your "business", do a "premiere"!

8TH
CHAPTER

PREPARE FOR SACRIFICES

If you just so happen to be reading this and you are a wife and a mother, I first would like to congratulate you on your achievement in preparing to "own your own" business! And that's the great news! Now for the challenge... Unfortunately, with any "growth" there are sacrifices; however, these sacrifices do not have to make everything operate in a "state of flux". Just as you must properly "prepare" in the scheduling and execution of your business, you must also do so in your home.

I, myself, have been associated in the business world of Entrepreneurship since birth. My Dad, SFC US ARMY Mr. John Ray Turner, after retiring from the military, gave back to his community, back in 1962 when he opened a convenience store called "Turner's Grocery and Gas". Well, in 1964, he and my Mom ushered me into the Earth's atmosphere and at the age of three years old, my Dad had me working in his store, stocking can goods, teaching me how to "front face" them for mass appeal. Now, I enjoyed working in that store when I was a child; however, it became something that I "dreaded" as a teenager; however, I now embrace and I am so grateful for everything that my Dad taught me.

I am saying that to say this... Ladies, you can do this... and it is no sin to own, operate and successfully run your own business, while being a wife and/or a mother, too. In fact if you have a Bible around or can access Biblehub.com, go to the book of **PROVERBS, chapter 31, and start at verse 10**. This is the story of a wife and mother who is referred to as VIRTUROUS! She is **H. E. R.** (*Hardworking, Empowered and Resilient*)! And she was an Entrepreneur! Take note on how she is described as a woman, a wife and a mother. Also, how her character and her business operations are described. Okay, here's the breakdown:

Biblehub.com – Proverbs 31:

   10) *"Who can find a wife with a strong character? She is worth far more than jewels.*

   11) *Her husband trusts her with [all] his heart, and he does not lack anything good.*

   12) *She helps him and never harms him all the days of her life.*

   13) *"She seeks out wool and linen [with care] and works with willing hands.*

   14) *She is like merchant ships. She brings her food from far away.*

   15) *She wakes up while it is still dark and gives food to her family and portions of food to her female* slaves *(employees).*

   16) *"She picks out a field and buys it. She plants a vineyard from the profits she has earned.*

17) She puts on strength like a belt and goes to work with energy.

18) She sees that she is making a good profit. Her lamp burns late at night.

19) "She puts her hands on the distaff, and her fingers hold a spindle.

20) She opens her hands to oppressed people and stretches them out to needy people.

21) She does not fear for her family when it snows because her whole family has a double layer of clothing.

22) She makes quilts for herself. Her clothes are [made of] linen and purple cloth.

23) "Her husband is known at the city gates when he sits with the leaders of the land.

24) "She makes linen garments and sells them and delivers belts to the merchants.

25) She dresses with strength and nobility, and she smiles at the future.

26) "She speaks with wisdom, and on her tongue there is tender instruction.

27) She keeps a close eye on the conduct of her family, and she does not eat the bread of idleness.

28) Her children and her husband stand up and bless her. In addition, he sings her praises, by saying,

29) 'Many women have done noble work, but you have surpassed them all!'

30) "Charm is deceptive, and beauty evaporates, [but] a woman who has [the fear of the LORD] (who embraces, enjoys, understands and cherishes LIFE) should be praised.

31) Reward her for what she has done, and let her achievements praise her at the city gates. God's Word Translation – Proverbs 12

Why reference the "Bible", you may ask? Well, this woman's life – this wife, this mother, this woman – is a historical symbol for all women who are, or would like to become Entrepreneurs while being a wife and mother. She shows us that even back over 4000+ years ago, she was not only smart, beautiful, generous, had business savvy, and a mogul in areas of International Trade, Warehousing, Import/Export, Marketing, Advertising, Manufacturing, Production, Sales, Counseling, Coaching, Training, Organization, Planning, Scheduling, Executing, etc., ... she takes care of her employees and she, on top of everything, is a great Wife and Mother, who has her house affairs in order as well!

Her schedule starts BEFORE anyone else gets up, and ends AFTER everyone else goes to bed... daily. Talk about POWER NAPS! Her "sacrifices" really aren't sacrifices, but "rewards" for being so RESPONSIBLE, so **H. E. R**.! She doesn't "dread" her life, because she "works" her passion. If you don't believe me, look at verse 25 where it states that she "smiles" at the future. Not any of those verses show her "frustrated", fearful, doubtful or worried about her family's or her future, because I believe that she was "too blessed to be stressed". She has too much she is and has to be responsible "for" and she doesn't have time to get "stressed" out. I believe that everything she did, she not only "loved" to do, but she was "passionate about doing them; thus, causing her COMFORT and JOY, not just about the present, but also the future. So much so, she SMILES! When was the last time that you "smiled" with the confidence in knowing that everything was going to be alright? When are you going to get rid of "fear, doubt and disbelief" and KNOW that you can DO THIS! Stop comparing yourself to "others"... let THEM compare themselves to you-verse 29!

Watch this... her husband "trusts her" with everything, emotionally, within himself; therefore, she "makes" time just for him. He is well known and has a high position. She makes time for her children – verse 27. In verse 28, her children and her husband praises her for her hard work and dedication.

She is a wife, mother, business mogul and a success.... She is a woman in every sense and aspect of the word... and **"YOU" CAN BE H. E. R. *(Hardworking Empowered and Resilient)* !**

ABOUT THE AUTHOR

Rhonda Gayle Turner Garner, 50 year old, wife and mother of six, has been in the world of business since the age of three. Introduced to the business world by her Dad, Mr. John Ray Turner – Retired SFC US ARMY for 21 years.

Being an only child of an Entrepreneur and a Teacher – her Mom, Mrs. Reba Smith Turner, retired – 30 years of service, Florence School District 4, Timmonsville, SC – Rhonda Gayle, as she is known by her family, inherited the spirit of them both.

She is a Timmonsville High School graduate in which she served on the Cheerleader squad as well as School Bus Driver. With degrees from Hampton Institute University – Hampton, VA B.A. Mass Media Arts – c/o 1986 / 1987 Graduate, American Intercontinental University Online – Buckhead, GA MBA Marketing – 2004 Graduate, American Intercontinental University MBA – Dual Degree – Accounting and Finance, Rhonda Gayle utilizes her degrees in her own business...The AdnohR Connection.

She is a TV Show Host on "Basic Life with Rhonda

Gayle", in which she also Produces, Directs and Engineers. She is also a Narrator for (Audible Audio Books) in which her profile can be found on ACX.com. An author, actress, Life Coach, Motivator, Encourager, Speaker, and BELIEVER in LOVE – LIFE – TRUTH, she chooses to be able to help all types of people. Rhonda Gayle is also the Founder of Hidden Truth Ministries in which her Passion is Encouraging Others to BE all that they can be and do all they can do to EVOLve into the person they were created to be.

COMFORT AND JOY be unto you all!

www.ingramcontent.com/pod-product-compliance
Lightning Source LLC
Chambersburg PA
CBHW040816200526
45159CB00024B/2993